March 2012

OPERATIONAL CONTRACT SUPPORT

Management and Oversight Improvements Needed in Afghanistan

GAO
Accountability * Integrity * Reliability

Highlights

Highlights of GAO-12-290, report to congressional committees

OPERATIONAL CONTRACT SUPPORT

Management and Oversight Improvements Needed in Afghanistan

Why GAO Did This Study

In fiscal year 2011, DOD reported obligating over $16 billion for contracts that were executed primarily in Afghanistan. GAO has previously identified the need for DOD to improve its oversight of contractors by non-acquisition personnel, such as CORs, and Congress has addressed this issue in legislation. CORs act as the liaisons between the contractor, the contracting officer, and the unit receiving support.

Following up on previous GAO work on this topic, GAO determined the extent to which (1) DOD's required training prepares CORs to perform their contract management and oversight duties, (2) CORs have the subject area-related technical expertise needed to oversee contracts, and (3) the number of CORs is sufficient to oversee the contracts in Afghanistan. GAO conducted field work in Afghanistan and the United States and focused on the preparedness of CORs to manage and oversee contracts in the CENTCOM area of responsibility.

What GAO Recommends

GAO recommends that DOD enhance the current strategy for managing and overseeing contracts in contingency areas such as Afghanistan by, for example, developing training standards for providing operational contract support (OCS), fully institutionalizing OCS in professional military education, and developing standards regarding the number of contracts that CORs can oversee based on the technical nature and complexity of the contract. DOD concurred with all of GAO's recommendations.

View GAO-12-290. For more information, contact Cary B. Russell at (404) 679-1808 or russellc@gao.gov

What GAO Found

The Department of Defense (DOD) has taken steps to enhance its existing training program for contracting officer's representatives (CORs), but the required training does not fully prepare them to perform their contract oversight duties in contingency areas such as Afghanistan. DOD requires that CORs be qualified by training and experience commensurate with the responsibilities to be delegated to them. DOD took several actions to enhance its training program, such as developing a CORs training course with a focus on contingency operations. However, GAO found that CORs are not prepared to oversee contracts because the required training does not include specifics on how to complete written statements of work and how to operate in Afghanistan's unique contracting environment. For example, DOD contracting personnel told GAO about opening delays and additional expenses related to the construction of a dining facility, which was originally constructed without a kitchen because it was not included in the original statement of work. In some cases, contract-specific training was not provided at all. In addition, not all oversight personnel such as commanders and senior leaders receive training to perform contract oversight and management duties in Afghanistan because such training is not required of them. Because DOD's required training does not prepare CORs and other oversight personnel to oversee contracts, units cannot be assured that they receive what they paid for.

CORs do not always have the necessary subject area-related technical expertise to oversee U.S. Central Command (CENTCOM) contracts they were assigned to. Contracting officials noted, for example, that the staircases on guard towers at a forward operating base were poorly constructed and unsafe to climb. The COR assigned to that contract had inadequate subject area-related technical expertise, preventing the early identification of the defective welding on the staircases. According to contracting officials, situations like this often occurred due to the shortage of CORs with expertise in construction. Also, at the time of GAO's field work, CORs for contracts written by CENTCOM contracting officers did not have access to subject matter experts, particularly those with construction experience. According to contracting personnel, because CORs do not have the subject area-related technical expertise needed to oversee contracts or access to subject matter experts, facilities were sometimes deficient and had to be reconstructed at great additional expense to the taxpayer.

DOD does not have a sufficient number of CORs to oversee the numerous contracts in Afghanistan. CENTCOM requires CORs to be nominated for all service contracts over $2,500 that, unless exempted, require significant ongoing technical advice and surveillance from requirements personnel. However, there is no guidance on the number of contracts a single COR should oversee. According to contracting officials and CORs GAO interviewed in Afghanistan, some CORs were responsible for providing oversight to multiple contracts in addition to carrying out their primary military duty. For example, one COR GAO interviewed was assigned to more than a dozen construction projects. According to that COR, it was impossible to be at each construction site during key phases of the project because the projects were occurring almost simultaneously at different locations. Consequently, according to officials, in situations like these, construction was completed without sufficient government oversight and problems were sometimes identified after facilities had been completed.

_____ **United States Government Accountability Office**

Contents

Abbreviations

C^3	CENTCOM Contracting Command
C-JTSCC	CENTCOM Joint Theater Support Contracting Command
CORs	contracting officer's representatives
COIN	counterinsurgency
DCMA	Defense Contract Management Agency
DOD	Department of Defense
FAR	Federal Acquisition Regulation
LOGCAP	Logistics Civil Augmentation Program
OCS	Operational Contract Support
SCO-A	Senior Contracting Official-Afghanistan
USD AT&L	Under Secretary of Defense for Acquisition, Technology and Logistics
CENTCOM	U.S. Central Command

United States Government Accountability Office
Washington, DC 20548

March 29, 2012

Congressional Committees

The Department of Defense (DOD) reported that it had obligated over $16 billion in fiscal year 2011 for contracts that were executed primarily in Afghanistan and that, as of October 2011, contractors made up 49 percent of the department's workforce there—101,789 DOD contractors[1] compared with approximately 104,900 U.S. military personnel. Contractors support the military during contingency operations[2] by, for example, managing dining facilities; washing uniforms; guarding military bases; constructing roads to schools; transporting supplies; and building facilities, such as guard towers, water treatment plants, and hospitals. Since 1997, we have reported on DOD's use of contractors to support contingency operations. For example, we reported in July 2004 that DOD did not always have sufficient contract oversight personnel to manage and oversee its logistics support contracts in Iraq and Afghanistan.[3] In December 2006, we noted that without an adequate number of trained oversight personnel DOD could not be assured that contractors could meet contract requirements efficiently and effectively.[4] Effective contract management is essential for ensuring that U.S. military personnel receive

---

[1]Office of the Deputy Assistant Secretary of Defense (Program Support), *Contractor Support of U.S. Operations in the USCENTCOM Area of Responsibility*, Quarterly Contractor Census Reports, October 2011. As we have noted in previous reports, however, agency-reported census data should not be used to identify trends or draw conclusions about the number of contractor personnel due to limitations such as incomplete and inaccurate data. *See GAO, Iraq and Afghanistan: DOD, State, and USAID Cannot Fully Account for Contracts, Assistance Instruments, and Associated Personnel*, GAO-11-886 (Washington, D.C.: Sept. 15, 2011).

[2]A "contingency operation" is a military operation that either (a) is designated by the Secretary of Defense as an operation in which members of the armed forces are or may become involved in military actions, operations, or hostilities against U.S. enemies or against an opposing military force or (b) results in the call or order to, or retention on, active duty of members of the uniformed services under certain statutory provisions or any other provision of law during a war or during a national emergency declared by the President or Congress. *See* 10 U.S.C. § 101(a)(13).

[3]GAO, *Military Operations: DOD's Extensive Use of Logistics Support Contracts Requires Strengthened Oversight*, GAO-04-854 (Washington, D.C.: July 21, 2004).

[4]GAO, *Military Operations: High-Level DOD Action Needed to Address Long-standing Problems with Management and Oversight of Contractors Supporting Deployed Forces*, GAO-07-145 (Washington, D.C.: Dec. 18, 2006).

the support they need and that controls are in place to prevent fraud, waste, and abuse. Ultimately, failure to manage contracts effectively could undermine U.S. policy objectives and threaten the safety of U.S. forces.

It takes a wide range of people to execute an acquisition from start to finish including personnel outside of the acquisition workforce such as contracting officer's representatives (CORs). CORs are military or civilian DOD personnel that manage and oversee contracts by acting as the eyes and the ears of DOD's contracting officers and by serving as the liaisons between the contractor, the contracting officer, and the unit receiving support or services. The contracting officer is ultimately responsible for ensuring that contractors meet the requirements as set forth in the contract. However, the CORs are non-acquisition personnel that have acquisition-related responsibilities—particularly those related to contract management and oversight of service and product acquisitions.

We and other oversight entities have identified the need for DOD to improve the management and oversight of contractors by non-acquisition personnel, such as the CORs. Congress addressed the need to improve the management and oversight of non-acquisition personnel, in legislation. Specifically, Congress included provisions relating to contingency contracting in the John Warner National Defense Authorization Act for Fiscal Year 2007[5] and the National Defense Authorization Act for Fiscal Year 2008,[6] codified at section 2333 of Title

---

[5]Pub. L. No. 109-364 (2006).

[6]Pub. L. No. 110-181 (2008).

10, United States Code.[7] The National Defense Authorization Act for Fiscal Year 2008 amended section 2333 to require that certain DOD joint policy provide for training of military personnel outside the acquisition workforce expected to have acquisition responsibility, including oversight duties during combat operations, post-conflict operations, and contingency operations.[8] Further, section 2333 requires that the training be sufficient to ensure that such military personnel understand the scope and scale of contractor support that they will experience in contingency operations and are prepared for their roles and responsibilities in regard to requirements definition, program management (including contractor oversight), and contingency contracting,[9] which are aspects of operational contract support (OCS). Specific concerns have been raised about the training, expertise, and the sufficiency of the number of CORs providing contract management and oversight. For example, in 2007, the Commission on Army Acquisition and Program Management in Expeditionary Operations (known as the Gansler Report) found that CORs usually had no experience managing contracts and received contract management training that was not relevant to the Afghanistan contracting environment.[10] Further, in June 2009, the Commission on Wartime Contracting reported shortfalls in the number of qualified oversight personnel in Afghanistan, specifically CORs, and a general lack

---

[7] See Pub. L. No. 109-364, § 854(a)(1); Pub. L. No. 110-181, § 849. The provision in the John Warner National Defense Authorization Act for Fiscal Year 2007 required the Secretary of Defense to develop joint policies addressing contingency contracting, among other matters. See Pub. L. No. 109-364, § 854(a)(1) (codified as amended at 10 U.S.C. § 2333(d)). Section 2333, as enacted by the provision, also defines "contingency contracting" as all stages of the process of acquiring property or services by the Department of Defense during a contingency operation. See 10 U.S.C. § 2333(f)(2). We reported in June 2010 that DOD had not yet finalized the joint policies required by Congress in the National Defense Authorization Acts for Fiscal Years 2007 and 2008. On December 20, 2011, DOD reissued Department of Defense Instruction 3020.41 with a new title—Operational Contract Support. The revised instruction establishes policy, assigns responsbilities, and provides procedures for OCS. DOD issued regulations with similar content in an interim final rule published in the Federal Register shortly thereafter. See Operational Contract Support, 76 Fed. Reg. 81,807 (Dec. 29, 2011) (to be codified at 32 C.F.R. pt. 158). We did not assess the recent issuances in this report.

[8] See Pub. L. No. 110-181, § 849(a)(2) (codified at 10 U.S.C. § 2333(e)).

[9] See § 2333(e)(2).

[10] Report of the "Commission on Army Acquisition and Program Management in Expeditionary Operations", *Urgent Reform Required: Army Expeditionary Contracting,* (Oct. 31, 2007).

of COR training.[11] Then, in August 2011, the Commission on Wartime Contracting reported that poor planning and oversight by the government and poor performance by contractors had resulted in wasted resources, missions not being achieved, and the loss of lives.[12] A recent U.S. Army Contracting Command article[13] noted that many deploying units were either unaware of, or simply ignored, a certain Army road map for units to follow to successfully integrate OCS training, including training CORs into its pre-deployment preparations; the article concluded that units continued to deploy unprepared to execute their OCS mission. We testified in June 2011 that, though DOD had taken some actions to better prepare CORs for their management and oversight duties, improving CORs' performance remained a challenge.[14]

Although CORs are non-acquisition personnel, they have acquisition-related responsibilities—particularly those related to contract management and oversight. In October 2010, in response to a mandate in the National Defense Authorization Act for Fiscal Year 2010,[15] we reported on training provided by the Defense Acquisition University to the acquisition workforce.[16] This review supplements the 2010 and other reports focusing on the preparedness of CORs, one such group of non-

---

[11]Commission on Wartime Contracting in Iraq and Afghanistan, *At What Cost? Contingency Contracting in Iraq and Afghanistan, Interim Report to Congress (June 2009)*.

[12]Commission on Wartime Contracting in Iraq and Afghanistan: *Transforming Wartime Contracting: Controlling Cost and Reducing Risks,* Final Report to Congress (Aug. 31, 2011).

[13]U.S. Army Contracting Command, ACC Today, *Professional Workforce Gansler Report Findings Help Prioritize Pre-deployment Contracting Planning,* by Major Hurcel I. Williams, 412th Contracting Support Brigade, summer 2011.

[14]*GAO, Operational Contract Support: Actions Needed to Address Contract Oversight and Vetting of Non-U.S. Vendors in Afghanistan,* GAO-11-771T *(Washington, D.C.: June 30, 2011).*

[15]*See* Pub. L. No. 111-84, § 1108(b)(2) (2009).

[16]GAO, *Defense Acquisition Workforce: DOD's Training Program Demonstrates Many Attributes of Effectiveness, but Improvement Is Needed,* GAO-11-22 (Washington, D.C.: Oct. 28, 2010). In GAO-11-22, the acquisition workforce was described with reference to the Defense Acquisition Workforce Improvement Act, Pub. L. No. 101-510, §§ 1201-1211 (1990) (codified as amended at 10 U.S.C. ch. 87); GAO, *Defense Acquisition Workforce: Better Identification, Development, and Oversight Needed for Personnel Involved in Acquiring Services,* GAO-11-892 (Washington, D.C.: Sept. 27, 2011). Following this work, in GAO-11-892 we examined personnel outside the workforce defined under the Defense Acquisition Workforce Improvement Act who are involved with acquiring services.

acquisition personnel, tasked with contract management and oversight responsibilities in Afghanistan. Specifically, our objectives were to determine the extent to which (1) DOD's required training prepares CORs to perform their contract management and oversight duties, (2) CORs have the subject area-related technical expertise needed to oversee contracts, and (3) the number of CORs is sufficient to oversee the contracts in Afghanistan.

To address our objectives, we assessed training requirements, technical qualifications, and workload requirements for CORs by reviewing guidance such as the Joint Publication 4-10,[17] the U.S. Central Command (CENTCOM) Joint Theater Support Contracting Command[18] Standard Operating Procedures addressing the Contracting Officer's Representative Program,[19] the Defense Contingency Contracting Officer's Representative Handbook, and the Joint Contingency Contracting Officer's Representative Handbook. We interviewed senior contracting personnel from the Office of the Secretary of Defense, the Joint Staff, the combatant commands, service headquarters, the Defense Contract Management Agency (DCMA), and defense universities to obtain a comprehensive understanding of what training was available for CORs performing contract-related duties in Afghanistan. To assess the content of the training, we attended a weeklong training course for CORs at Fort Carson, Colorado, and completed the Defense Acquisition University's online CORs contingency courses. We also reviewed the program of instructions (course syllabus) for the training curriculum. In Afghanistan, we conducted interviews with over 150 DOD personnel (commanders, senior leaders, contracting personnel, and CORs) from over 30 defense organizations and units in Bagram, Kabul, Kandahar, and Camp Leatherneck to identify the extent to which DOD's required training had prepared CORs to perform their management and oversight duties, CORs had the subject area-related technical expertise needed to oversee contracts, and the number of CORs was sufficient to oversee the contracts in Afghanistan. We selected defense organizations and units to

---

[17] Joint Chiefs of Staff, Joint Pub. 4-10, Operational Contract Support (Oct. 17, 2008) (Hereinafter cited as Joint Pub. 4-10 (Oct. 17, 2008)). According to senior Army officials, Joint Publication 4-10 is doctrine, not policy and it is prescriptive in nature.

[18] Also known as CENTCOM Contracting Command (C³)

[19] CENTCOM Contracting Command Standard Operating Procedure No. 10-02: Contracting Officer's Representative (COR) Program (Rev. 2, June 2010).

interview that would be in Afghanistan and available during the time of our visit based on input from service officials as well as status reports from the U.S. Army, the U.S. Air Force, and the U.S. Army National Guard. To facilitate our meetings with CORs and contracting personnel in Afghanistan, we developed a set of structured questions that we pre-tested and coordinated with service contracting experts to ensure that we solicited the appropriate responses. See appendix I for our scope and methodology and a list of defense organizations and units we visited during the course of this engagement.

We conducted our work from April 2010 to March 2012 in accordance with generally accepted government auditing standards. Those standards require that we plan and perform the audit to obtain sufficient and appropriate evidence to serve as a basis for our findings and conclusions. We believe that the evidence that we have obtained serves as a reasonable basis for our findings and conclusions based on our audit objectives.

Background

"Oversight of a contract"—which can refer to contract administration functions, quality assurance surveillance, corrective action, property administration, and past performance evaluation—ultimately rests with the contracting officer who has the responsibility for ensuring that contractors meet the requirements set forth in the contract. However, contracting officers are frequently not located in the area or at the installation where the services are being provided. For that reason, contracting officers designate CORs via an appointment letter[20] to assist with the technical monitoring or administration of a contract on their behalf. CORs serve as the eyes and ears for the contracting officer and act as the liaisons between the contractor, the contracting officer, and the unit receiving support or services. CORs are responsible for tasks identified in the contracting officer's appointment letter that may include (1) providing daily contract oversight, (2) performing quality assurance reviews, (3) monitoring contract performance, and (4) assessing technical performance. CORs cannot direct the contractor by making commitments or changes that affect price, quality, quantity, delivery, or other terms and

---

[20]An appointment letter, or letter of designation, specifies among other things the extent of the COR's authority to act on behalf of the contracting officer, identifies limitations on the COR's authority, and specifies the period covered by the designation.

conditions of the contract. [21] In addition to their oversight duties, CORs have also been tasked with other contract-related duties such as preparing statements of work, which provide the requirements or specifications of the contract, developing requirements approval paperwork, and preparing funding documents. Although CORs are non-acquisition personnel, they can have acquisition-related responsibilities—particularly those related to contract oversight. CORs are not usually contracting specialists and often perform contract management and oversight duties on a part-time basis in addition to performing their primary military duties, such as those performed by an infantryman or a quartermaster specialist.

The Office of the Under Secretary of Defense for Acquisition, Technology, and Logistics (USD AT&L) has responsibility for developing overarching DOD policy for the management and oversight of contingency contracts.[22] For some contracts, including all contracts under the Logistics Civil Augmentation Program (LOGCAP),[23] according to officials, contracting officers may delegate contract administration to DCMA to monitor contractor performance. The DCMA teams in Afghanistan include (1) administrative contracting officers who administer contracts and often direct contractors to perform work and (2) quality assurance representatives who ensure that the contractors perform work to the standards written in the contracts and who oversee certain aspects of the performance of CORs assigned to DCMA-administered contracts. The DCMA team also includes property administrators and subject matter experts who advise the agency on technical issues such as food service, electrical engineering, and fire safety. However, construction contracts in Afghanistan are generally administered by personnel from the Army Corps of Engineers, or they may be administered by CENTCOM Joint

---

[21]CORs may also not be delegated responsibility to perform functions at a contractor's location that have been delegated to a contract administration office. *See* 48 C.F.R. § 201.602-2(2)(iii) (Defense Federal Acquisition Regulation Supplement).

[22]DOD defines the term "contingency contract" as a legally binding agreement for supplies, services, and construction let by government contracting officers in the operational area, as well as other contracts that have a prescribed area of performance within a designated operational area. These contracts include theater support, external support, and systems support contracts.

[23]LOGCAP is a program that provides worldwide logistics and base and life support services in contingency environments and provides the majority of base and life support services to U.S. forces in Iraq and Afghanistan.

Theater Support Contracting Command contracting officers assisted by CORs. When DCMA is not designated responsibility for administrative oversight of a contract, the contracting officer who awarded the contract is responsible for the administration, management, and oversight of the contract. These contracting officers, such as those from the CENTCOM Joint Theater Support Contracting Command often appoint CORs to monitor contractor performance.[24] CORs appointed by the CENTCOM Joint Theater Support Contracting Command are typically drawn from units receiving contractor-provided services. In Afghanistan, CORs that have been appointed to contracts administered by DCMA report oversight results to DCMA personnel. For contracts not administered by DCMA, CORs provide oversight information to the contracting officer. In Afghanistan, the CENTCOM Joint Theater Support Contracting Command directs requiring activities (units receiving contractor-provided goods and services) to nominate CORs for all service contracts valued at more than $2,500 with significant technical requirements that require ongoing advice and surveillance from technical/requirements personnel. The contracting officer may exempt service contracts from this requirement when the following three conditions are all met:

(1) The contract will be awarded using simplified acquisition procedures;

(2) The requirement is not complex; and

(3) The contracting officer documents the file, in writing, as to why the appointment of a COR is unnecessary.[25]

---

[24]Although the CENTCOM Joint Theater Support Contracting Command (C-JTSCC) commander is accountable for contract administration of all DOD contracts requiring contractors to deploy to theater to support operations, non-C-JTSCC theater support contracts that are not delegated to DCMA may be re-delegated back to the originator. See CENTCOM Joint Theater Support Contracting Command Acquisition Instruction § 25.7700(a) (Sept. 1, 2011).

[25]See CENTCOM Contracting Command Standard Operating Procedure No. 10-02: Contracting Officer's Representative (COR) Program ¶ 4(A) (Rev. 2, June 2010). A revised version of this guidance was released while this report was in its final stages; we did not have the opportunity to assess this guidance. As such, we refer in this report to the guidance that was in effect during the period of our review.

DOD Took Steps to Enhance Existing Training Program, but Existing Training Does Not Fully Prepare CORs for Contract Management and Oversight Duties

Although DOD requires CORs to receive training and took some actions to enhance training programs, CORs we met with in Afghanistan do not always receive adequate training to prepare them for their contract management and oversight duties. DOD requires that CORs be qualified by training and experience commensurate with the responsibilities to be delegated to them. According to DOD officials, the current training might qualify CORs to monitor contractor performance generally, but it does not necessarily make them sufficiently capable for their particular assignments. DOD officials have acknowledged gaps in training. For example, required DOD training taken by CORs did not fully address the unique contracting environment that exists in Afghanistan, which includes large numbers of Afghan contractors with limited experience and qualifications. Further, the instability and security aspects of remote locations throughout Afghanistan coupled with an undeveloped infrastructure impedes the CORs' ability to communicate with and rely upon acquisition personnel, such as contracting officers, for support and guidance. Additionally, not all of the required training for CORs was conducted, and some other oversight personnel were not being trained.

CORs Are Required to Receive Training and DOD Took Some Actions to Enhance Existing Training Programs

In Afghanistan, much of the daily surveillance of contractors supporting military operations is performed by CORs. The Federal Acquisition Regulation (FAR) requires that quality assurance, such as surveillance, be performed at such times and places as may be necessary to determine that the supplies or services conform to contract requirements. [26] DOD guidance requires CORs to be trained and assigned prior to award of a contract. DOD training is intended to familiarize the CORs with the duties and responsibilities of contract management and oversight. Contracting organizations such as the CENTCOM Joint Theater Support Contracting Command require that personnel nominated to be CORs complete specific online training courses [27] (referred to as Phase I), as well as locally developed CORs overview training, and contract-specific training provided by contracting officers in theater (the latter referred to as

---

[26] This surveillance generally involves government oversight of contractors with the purpose of ensuring that the contractor (the service provider) performs the requirements of the contract and the government (the service receiver or customer) receives the service as intended.

[27] Online CORs training was provided by the Defense Acquisition University; and the Army offers an on-line course for deployed CORs, which covered the same information as the 40-hour course provided by the Army Logistics University.

Phase II) before they can serve as CORs in Afghanistan. The guidance notes that, at a minimum, Phase II training will consist of contract specific responsibilities, including file documentation; terms and conditions of the contract; specifics of the performance work statement; acceptance of services procedures; invoice procedures; technical requirements; monthly reporting procedures, and contractor evaluation—all specific to their assigned contract.

DOD has taken some actions to enhance training programs to prepare CORs to manage and oversee contracts in contingency operations, such as in Afghanistan. For example, DOD developed a new training course for CORs, with a focus on contingency operations and developed a more general certification program for CORs, including the contingency operations course as a training requirement when it is applicable.[28] DOD also took steps to institutionalize operational contract support by including some CORs-related training in professional military education programs and by emphasizing the need for qualified CORs by discussing their responsibilities in joint doctrine and other guidance with the publication of Joint Publication 4-10—Operational Contract Support and the Defense Contingency Contracting Officer's Representative Handbook and memoranda issued by the Deputy Secretary of Defense.

Available DOD Training Does Not Fully Prepare CORs to Oversee Contracts in Afghanistan

Our analysis of DOD's CORs training and interviews with over 150 CORs and contracting personnel from over 30 defense organizations like the regional contracting centers[29] and the DCMA in Bagram, Kabul, Kandahar, and Camp Leatherneck, Afghanistan, indicated that some gaps and limitations existed in DOD's training programs leaving CORs not fully prepared to perform their contract management and oversight

---

[28]In addition to DOD actions, there are other similar government-wide efforts to revamp federal CORs policies. In September 2011, the Office of Federal Procurement Policy issued a memorandum describing revisions to the Federal Acquisition Certification for CORs. The purpose of the program, which applies to all executive agencies except DOD, is to establish general training, experience, and development requirements for CORs that reflect the various types of contracts they manage. *See* Memorandum from Daniel I. Gordon, Administrator, Office of Federal Procurement Policy, Revisions to the Federal Acquisition Certification for Contracting Officer's Representatives (FAC-COR) (Sept. 6, 2011).

[29]Regional Contracting Centers are involved in planning, coordinating, and managing theater support contracting for deployed U.S. forces and multinational forces support in Afghanistan.

duties. For example, the training for CORs is generally focused on low-risk contract operations in Afghanistan and does not fully address the unique contracting environment that exists there, such as the extent of inexperience of Afghan contractors, the remote and insecure locations of project sites, the underdeveloped infrastructure, and constraints on the movement and deployment of oversight personnel, especially acquisition personnel. More specifically, the required CORs training does not include information about important issue areas like the Afghan First Program, which encourages an increased use of local personnel and vendors for supplies and services as part of the U.S. counterinsurgency[30] strategy, and working with private security contractors. Some CORs in Afghanistan told us they were unaware of the challenges in working with Afghan contractors and thought contracting with them would be similar to contracting with U.S. vendors. However, according to some of the CORs and other contracting personnel we interviewed, providing oversight of Afghan contractors was more challenging than was the case with other vendors because the Afghan contractors often did not meet the timelines specified in the contract, did not provide the quality products and the services the units had anticipated, and did not necessarily have a working knowledge of English. Further, these officials told us that Afghan contractors were not always familiar with the business standards and processes of the U.S. government. For example, one COR told us during our visit in February 2011 that a unit was still waiting for barriers that it had contracted for in May 2010. According to that COR, while some of the barriers had been delivered, the unit had not received all of the barriers it required even though the contract delivery date had passed. Other CORs, contracting officials, and commanders described similar situations in which services were either not provided as anticipated or were not provided at all. Because of gaps in training, CORs did not always understand the full scope of their responsibilities and did not always ensure that the contractor was meeting all contract requirements. As a result, according to contracting officials, items such as portable toilets, gates, water, and other items or services were not available when needed, raising concerns about security, readiness, and morale.

Contracting officials from over 30 defense organizations and units in Bagram, Kabul, Kandahar, and Camp Leatherneck whom we spoke with

---

[30]Commander, International Security Assistance Force/United States Forces—Afghanistan, *COMISAF's Counterinsurgency (COIN) Contracting Guidance* (Sept. 8, 2010).

noted similar problems with construction contracts awarded to Afghan contractors. For example, according to another COR, an Afghan contractor was awarded a $70,000 contract to build a latrine, shower, and sink unit. The COR told us that the contractor was unable to satisfactorily complete the project and so another contract was awarded for approximately $130,000 to bring the latrine, shower, and sink unit to a usable condition. Because of inadequacies in training, CORs did not always understand that they had the responsibility to ensure that the terms of the contract were met and therefore did not bring contractors' performance issues to the contracting officer's attention for resolution. Similarly, DOD contracting officials provided us with documentation of other construction problems, including a shower/toilet facility built without holes in the walls or floors for plumbing and drain (fig. 1), and facilities that were constructed with poor-quality materials such as crumbling cement blocks (fig. 2).[31] The Special Inspector General for Afghanistan Reconstruction[32] has also reported significant construction deficiencies related to contracting in Afghanistan, including poorly formed and crumbling cement structures attributable to the lack of CORs training and oversight.

[31]The photographs in this report were selected from photographs provided by DOD personnel and were not necessarily a representation of the contract environment in Afghanistan. Any construction problems or other defects identified in the photographs are derived from statements from officials or DOD documentation.

[32]Special Inspector General Afghanistan Reconstruction, *ANP District Headquarters Facilities in Helmand and Kandahar Provinces Have Significant Construction Deficiencies Due to Lack of Oversight and Poor Contractor Performance* (Oct. 27, 2010).

Figure 1: Shower/Toilet Facility Constructed without Holes in the Walls or Flooring for Plumbing and Drain

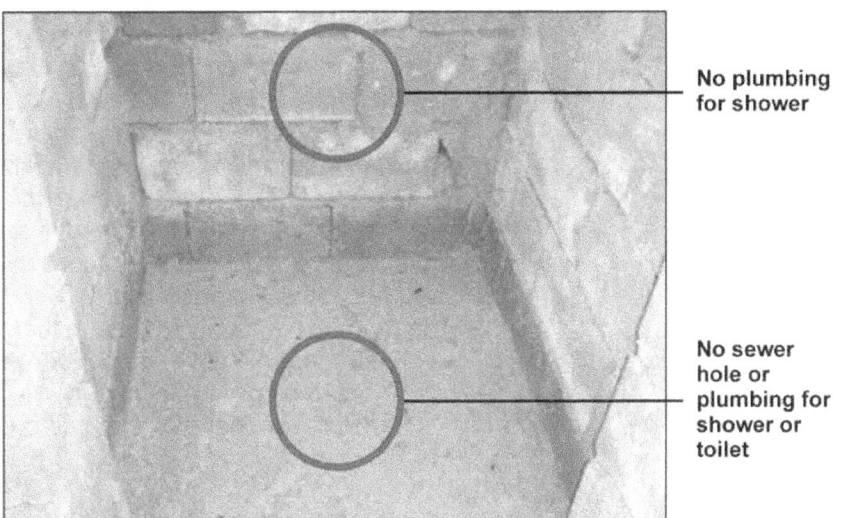

No plumbing for shower

No sewer hole or plumbing for shower or toilet

Source: Photograph and annotations provided by DOD personnel in Afghanistan.

Figure 2: Poor-Quality Materials—Crumbling Cement Blocks

Crumbling cement blocks

Source: Photograph and annotations provided by DOD personnel in Afghanistan.

Because of the nature and sensitivity of security contracts, CORs for private security contractors' contracts have unique responsibilities. For example, during the period of our review, under guidance in place prior to June 2011, CORs were responsible for compiling a monthly weapons discharge report and for ensuring contractor adherence to contractual obligations on topics such as civilian arming requirements, personnel reporting systems, property accountability, and identification badges. According to a senior military officer with U.S. Forces Afghanistan's private security contractor task force, because of gaps in training, CORs did not always understand the full scope of their responsibilities and so did not always ensure that a contractor was meeting all contract requirements. He noted that CORs did not always understand that they had the responsibility to ensure that the terms of the contract were met and therefore did not bring contractors' performance issues to the contracting officer's attention for resolution. As a result, DOD may pay contractors for poor performance and installations might not receive the level of security contracted for.

Further, we found that the training programs lacked specifics on the preparation of statements of work or documents required for acquisition review boards—two contract management responsibilities that CORs in Afghanistan were routinely tasked to do. Although the development of a statement of work involves a variety of participants from the contracting process, a COR may be uniquely suited to have an early impact on the development of a complete and accurate statement of work. The Defense Contingency Contracting Officer's Representative Handbook describes statements of work as specifying the basic top-level objectives of the acquisition as well as the detailed requirements of the government. The statement of work can provide the contractor with "how to" instructions to accomplish the required work. It could provide a detailed description of what is expected of the contractor and forms part of the basis for successful performance by the contractor and effective oversight of contracts by the government. Well-written statements of work are needed to ensure that units get the services and goods needed in the required time frame. As we reported in 2000 and 2004, poorly written statements of work can also increase costs and the number of substandard supplies and services provided by the contractor.[33] Based on discussions with

---

[33]GAO, *Military Operations: DOD's Extensive Use of Logistics Support Contracts Requires Strengthened Oversight*, GAO-04-854 (Washington, D.C.: July 19, 2004).

contracting personnel from four major bases in Afghanistan responsible for reviewing these documents, statements of work prepared by CORs were vague and lacked the specifics needed to provide units with what they wanted. We were told by multiple DOD officials that some CORs routinely cut and paste information from previous statements of work into their current document without adapting it as needed, resulting in errors that have to be corrected and further extending the time involved in procuring a good or service. Contracting personnel told us of instances in which statements of work had to be rewritten because the original statements of work did not include all the required contractor actions, or because they included incorrect requirements. Although there are other DOD contracting personnel involved in the requirement and procurement process, CORs can help to ensure that well-articulated needs are more fully documented at an early stage. DOD contracting personnel responsible for reviewing and approving requests for contract support told us that poorly written statements of work were a principal reason units do not receive the operational contract support they need for sustaining military operations. Because of gaps in training, CORs were unable to prepare well-articulated statements of work that clearly define the warfighters' needs. For example, DOD contracting personnel told us about a dining facility in Afghanistan that was built without a kitchen because it was not included in the original statement of work, resulting in DOD having to generate a separate statement of work for the kitchen. According to contracting officials and commanders, poorly written statements of work increase the procurement process time, the workload burden on the DOD contracting personnel, and delays and disruptions in critical supplies and services needed for the mission.

Moreover, according to DOD, one of the acquisition review boards in Afghanistan, known as the Joint Acquisition Review Board, reviews and recommends approval or disapproval of proposed acquisitions to ensure efficiency and cost effectiveness.[34] DOD contracting personnel responsible for reviewing acquisition proposals told us that delays and disruptions in supplies and services needed by the unit have been

---

[34]As described in Joint Publication 4-10, the Joint Acquisition Review Board's main role is to make specific approval and prioritization recommendations for all geographic combatant commander directed, subordinate joint force commander controlled, high-value and/or high-visibility common user logistics requirements, and to include recommendations on the proper source of support for these requirements. *See* Joint Pub. 4-10 (Oct. 17, 2008).

GAO-12-290 Operational Contract Support

attributed to incomplete or incorrect documents, such as statements of work. Since CORs in Afghanistan are heavily relied upon by their units and the acquisition personnel in the development of these documents, it is important that they understand what paperwork is required and how to properly complete it in order to obtain needed goods and services in a timely manner. Contracting officials acknowledge the challenges with preparing complete/correct statements of work and DOD is making some effort to address the gaps in training. For example, the Defense Acquisition University provides a training course on preparing requirements documents such as statements of work; however, it is not a DOD requirement for CORs and contracting personnel to complete this training before assuming their contract-related roles and responsibilities.

Not All CORs Receive Required Training

DOD contracting personnel and CORs in Afghanistan told us that the CENTCOM Joint Theater Support Contracting Command contracting officers were frequently unable to provide the required contract-specific training (Phase II) for CORs because they were busy awarding contracts. For instance, a COR whom we interviewed in Afghanistan was directing a contractor to perform construction work or correct deficiencies in performance without authorization from or communication with the contracting officer. Because the COR had never received the required training from the contracting officer, he was not aware that this practice was potentially unauthorized. Without the follow-on Phase II training from the contracting officer, CORs may lack a clear and full understanding of the scope of their contract duties and responsibilities. In contrast, DCMA's contracting personnel provide specific contract training and mentoring to its CORs because DCMA has full-time quality assurance personnel who have been tasked with providing COR training and assistance. According to DCMA officials, certified quality assurance representatives continue to mentor CORs after their formal training has been completed.

Moreover, in addition to CORs, other personnel expected to perform contract oversight and management duties in Afghanistan are not always being trained. Joint Publication 4-10 states that military departments are responsible for ensuring that military personnel outside the acquisition workforce who are expected to have acquisition responsibility, including oversight duties associated with contracts or contractors are properly trained.[35] The Joint Publication also highlights the key role of

---

[35] *See* Joint Pub. 4-10 at II-8 (Oct. 17, 2008).

GAO-12-290 Operational Contract Support

commanders and senior leaders in operational contract support oversight. However, contracting personnel that we interviewed in Afghanistan told us that military personnel such as commanders and senior leaders did not always receive training on their contract management and oversight duties in Afghanistan and that commanders, particularly those in combat units, do not perceive operational contract support as a warfighter task.[36] Although some contracting-related training is available for commanders and senior leaders, it is not required before deployment. DOD has not expanded the professional military education curriculum by increasing the number of training offerings on operational contract support with a particular emphasis on contingency operations to fully institutionalize operational contract support in professional military education. Based on our previous findings, it is essential that commanders and senior leaders complete operational contract support training before deployment to avoid confusion regarding their contract role and responsibilities in managing and overseeing contractors, and nominating qualified CORs. In 2006, we recommended that operational contract support training be included in the professional military education to ensure that all military personnel expected to perform contract management duties, including commanders and senior leaders, receive training prior to deployment. DOD has taken some actions to implement this recommendation by developing some Programs of Instruction on contingency acquisition for their non-acquisition workforce to be taught at some of the military and senior staff colleges. However, commanders and senior leaders are not required to take these courses before assuming their contract management and oversight roles and responsibilities.

---

[36]Commanders and senior leaders generally lack the authority to enter into contracts or otherwise direct contractors or contract performance. However, as noted in Joint Publication 4-10, these personnel play a key role in determining specific contracted support requirements, contracting planning, and execution of OCS oversight, which we include here in the term "contract management and oversight."

CORs Do Not Always Have the Subject Area-Related Technical Expertise Needed to Oversee Some Contracts

CORs did not always have the subject area-related technical expertise or access to subject matter experts with those skills to manage and oversee contracts in Afghanistan, especially those contracts of a highly technical and complex nature. The Defense Contingency Contracting Officer's Representative Handbook indicates that CORs are responsible for determining whether products delivered or services rendered by the contractor conform to the requirements for the service or commodity covered under the contract. Further, the Contracting Officer's Representative Handbook notes that CORs should have technical expertise related to the requirements covered by the contract.

However, according to CORs and contracting personnel we interviewed in Afghanistan, CORs did not have the subject area-related technical expertise necessary to monitor contract performance for the contracts they were assigned to oversee. For example, many of these CORs were appointed to oversee construction contracts without the necessary engineering or construction experience, in part because their units lacked personnel with those technical skills. While DCMA had subject matter experts in key areas such as fire safety available for CORs needing technical assistance, CORs for contracts written by the CENTCOM Joint Theater Support Contracting Command did not have subject matter experts to turn to for assistance, particularly in the construction trades during the time of our visit. As a result, according to officials, there were newly constructed buildings that had to be repaired or rebuilt before being used by U.S. and Afghan troops because the CORs providing the oversight were not able to adequately ensure proper construction. According to personnel we interviewed, these practices resulted in wasted resources, low morale, and risks to the safety of base and installation personnel where the deficient guard towers, fire stations, and gates were constructed. Officials stated that it is not uncommon for a COR to accept a portion of the contractor's work only to find later upon further examination that the work was not in accordance with the contract and substandard. Similarly, officials stated that the LOGCAP personnel did not accept responsibility for maintenance of a facility that had been constructed by Afghan contractors until LOGCAP contractors first repaired or replaced wiring and plumbing to meet building codes. Although the CORs were not solely responsible for contract oversight, or for the implications identified above, they could have provided an early verification of contractor performance. More importantly, in the Afghanistan contracting environment the DOD contracting personnel ultimately responsible for oversight—such as contracting officers—were often removed or absent from the remote locations where the work was performed and had no ability to communicate electronically. This results in greater reliance on CORs and reduces the opportunity for CORs to identify problems early in the process. The following were cases that further illustrate the impact of CORs not having the technical skills or support needed to perform contract management and oversight. Although the CORs did not necessarily bear the sole responsibility for consequences identified below, a well-trained COR might have been able to prevent or mitigate the effects of the problems.

- According to officials, a COR prepared a statement of work for a contract to build floors and install tents but failed to include any power requirements necessary to run air conditioners, heaters, and lights because the COR and unit personnel did not have the electrical technical expertise to properly and safely specify the correct power converter package[37] with the original request. Thus, the tents were unusable until the unit used a field ordering officer to order, at an additional cost, the correct power converters so that the tents were usable and completed in a timely fashion.
- Contracting officials told us that guard towers at a forward operating base were poorly constructed and unsafe to occupy. As shown in figure 3, the staircase was unstable and not strong enough for climbing; it had to be torn down and reconstructed. The COR's inadequate subject area-related technical expertise or access to subject matter experts prevented the early identification of defective welding on the staircase that rendered it unsuitable to use to climb up the guard tower.

---

[37]A power converter package comprises a fuse box, electrical wiring and other electrical materials enabling connection to a power supply such as a generator, to run air conditioners, heaters, and lights in the tents.

Figure 3: Unstable Staircase for Guard Towers

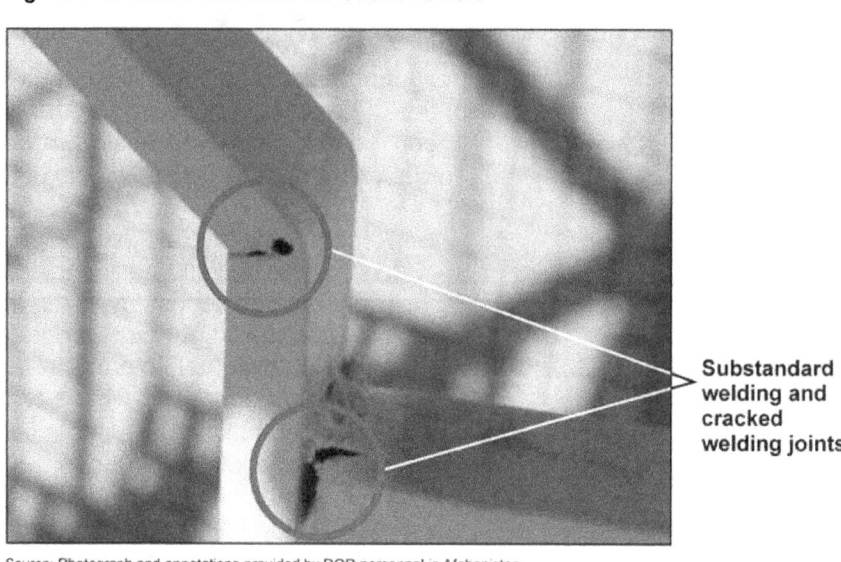

Substandard welding and cracked welding joints

Source: Photograph and annotations provided by DOD personnel in Afghanistan.

- A senior engineer inspector official told us the cement block walls that had been accepted by a COR were poorly constructed. The COR did not have the subject area-related technical expertise or access to subject matter experts necessary to properly inspect and reject substandard cement block walls. For example, the contracting official noted large holes in a cement block wall that remained after the wood scaffolding was removed, which rendered the wall unstable (fig. 4).

Figure 4: Cement Block Wall with Large Holes That Remained When Scaffolding Was Removed

Large holes in block wall left from scaffolding

Source: Photograph and annotations provided by DOD personnel in Afghanistan.

- A dining facility expected to service 1,000 military personnel was unused for a year due to emergent construction deficiencies such as electrical and plumbing issues. Contracting officials attributed the construction issues to the shortage of oversight personnel with subject area-related technical expertise or access to subject matter experts in construction. As a result, according to contracting personnel, repair work to correct the deficiencies was acquired under LOGCAP for $190,000 in addition to the original cost of the contract.

The issue of CORs not having adequate subject area-related technical expertise has been a longstanding problem in DOD. For example, we have previously reported in 2006, 2008, and again in 2010 that CORs do not always have the subject area-related technical expertise necessary to oversee contracts.[38] More recently in November and August 2011, the Congressional Research Service and the Commission on Wartime Contracting in Iraq and Afghanistan reported that DOD is still in need of non-acquisition personnel with the necessary technical and subject matter

---

[38]GAO-07-145, GAO-08-1087, and GAO-10-472.

GAO-12-290 Operational Contract Support

expertise to perform contractor oversight, respectively.[39] The Special Inspector General for Afghanistan Reconstruction[40] has also reported significant construction deficiencies with contracting in Afghanistan as a result of inadequate subject area-related technical expertise on the part of CORs and other contract oversight personnel. Problem areas identified by the Inspector General included low-quality concrete (similar to conditions depicted in fig. 2 and fig. 4) and inadequate roofing installations, which were similar to other deficiencies we identified.

Further, based on DOD documentation, the nature of contract work in Afghanistan has become more technical and complex, increasing the number of CORs needed, the amount of time needed to award contracts, and the number of errors during the early stages of the contracting process (e.g., the requirements determination process). Due to the complexity of construction projects in Afghanistan, DOD established an initiative in April 2011 to assign construction inspectors to assist CORs in managing and overseeing construction projects. According to a DOD memorandum,[41] contracting officers should appoint construction inspectors, in addition to CORs, when the nature of the project requires technical assistance to ensure proper performance of work and when such assistance is available. Because this program was not in effect during the time of our visit in February 2011, we are unable to assess the effectiveness of the use of construction inspectors. However, based on our observations in Afghanistan, there is a shortage of subject area-related technical experts that can serve as construction inspectors in Afghanistan. CORs and other personnel that we interviewed in Afghanistan acknowledged the benefit of having subject matter experts in construction as well as other specialty areas such as food-, fuel-, and electricity-related services.

---

[39]Congressional Research Service, Report Number R42084, *Wartime Contracting in Afghanistan: Analysis and Issues for Congress,* by Moshe Schwartz, November 14, 2011 and Commission on Wartime Contracting in Iraq and Afghanistan, *Transforming Wartime Contracting: Controlling Cost and Reducing Risks,* Final Report to Congress, August 2011.

[40]Special Inspector General Afghanistan Reconstruction, *ANP District Headquarters Facilities in Helmand and Kandahar Provinces Have Significant Construction Deficiencies Due to Lack of Oversight and Poor Contractor Performance,* October 27, 2010.

[41]Senior Contracting Official-Afghanistan (SCO-A), *Memorandum for SCO-A Contracting Officers-Inspector Duties for Construction Contractors* (Apr. 27, 2011).

Number of CORs Is Not Sufficient to Adequately Oversee the Contracts in Afghanistan

DOD does not have a sufficient number of CORs to oversee the numerous contracts in Afghanistan[42] and, according to some government officials, there are not enough CORs in theatre to conduct adequate oversight.[43] The CENTCOM Joint Theater Support Contracting Command requires the nomination of CORs for all service contracts worth over $2,500 with significant technical requirements that require on-going advice and surveillance from technical or requirements personnel, unless exempted by the contracting officer.[44] Although there is no specific guidance on the number of contracts a single COR should manage, the CENTCOM Joint Theater Support Contracting Command requires that CORs nominations signed by the unit commander contain a statement verifying that the CORs will have sufficient time to perform assigned tasks. Similarly, the Defense Contingency Contracting Officer's Representative Handbook states that the requiring unit must allow adequate resources (time, products, equipment, and opportunity) for the CORs to perform their functions. In 2004, 2006, and again in 2010, we reported that the DOD did not have a sufficient number of trained oversight personnel, and during the course of our review we noted that this situation persisted. Further, we found that CORs do not always have the time needed to complete their oversight responsibilities. While available data do not enable us to determine the precise number of contracts that require CORs, in fiscal year 2011, DOD completed over 35,000 contracting actions on over 24,600 contracts and orders that were

---

[42]We did not review every contract in Afghanistan managed by CORs. Our findings were based on information obtained from DOD contracting personnel in Afghanistan—units that we selected based on availability.

[43]Congressional Research Service, Report Number R42084, *Wartime Contracting in Afghanistan: Analysis and Issues for Congress*, by Moshe Schwartz, November 14, 2011, p.5.

[44]Contracting officers may exempt service contracts from the requirement when the following three conditions are met: (1) the contract will be awarded using simplified acquisition procedures; (2) the requirement is not complex; and (3) the contracting officer documents the file, in writing why the appointment of a COR is unnecessary.

GAO-12-290 Operational Contract Support

executed primarily in Afghanistan.[45] According to contracting officials and CORs we interviewed in Afghanistan, some CORs are responsible for providing oversight to multiple contracts in addition to performing their primary military duty. For example, one COR we interviewed was assigned to more than a dozen construction projects. According to the COR, it was impossible to be at each construction site during key phases of the project, such as for the concrete pouring of building footings, wiring installation, or plumbing. Consequently, according to contracting officials, construction on these multiple projects was completed without sufficient government oversight and problems were not always identified until the building was completed. This often resulted in significant rework, at a cost to the U.S. taxpayer.

In another instance, an entire compound of five buildings was built in the wrong location. According to DOD, based on the statement of work, the compound should have been constructed on base behind the security walls but instead was constructed outside the perimeter of the base in a non-secure location. Contracting officials we spoke with in Afghanistan attributed the problem to the numerous contracts managed by the COR and the lack of time to perform contract oversight duties. As a result, according to officials, the buildings (shown in fig. 5) could not be used. The cost of the compound including the five buildings was $2.4 million.

[45]Data based on GAO analysis of Federal Procurement Database System-Next Generation Data as of January 2012. The number of contracts includes stand-alone contracts for goods and services, as well as purchase, delivery, and task orders; Blanket Purchase Agreements and Indefinite Delivery/Indefinite Quantity contracts are not included, but the orders under them are. The number of contract actions includes contracts and orders awarded or modified where the place of performance was identified as Afghanistan. Federal Procurement Database System-Next Generation Data includes unclassified contracts that are estimated to be $3,000 or more and any modifications to these contracts regardless of dollar value. Although modifications do not themselves necessarily require the appointment of a new COR, they may indicate contract activity that would necessitate continued COR involvement.

Figure 5: Compound Comprising Five Buildings Constructed in a Non-Secure Location outside the Perimeter of a Base

Complex built outside of perimeter fence

Perimeter fence

Source: Photograph and annotations provided by DOD personnel in Afghanistan.

In addition, in some cases units did not assign enough CORs to provide oversight. For example, we were told by one unit that it did not have a sufficient number of CORs to provide proper oversight of dining facility services, including ordering and inspecting food and supplies. Although the unit was able to provide one COR for each dining facility, the dining facilities operate 24 hours a day. Contracting officials expressed concern that there were not enough CORs to provide sufficient oversight of the dining facilities 24 hours a day during all shifts of operation.

A significant factor that might contribute to a shortage of CORs is that contract oversight is often assigned a lower priority for units than tasks associated with their primary missions. Army officials stated that commanders, particularly those in combat units, do not perceive contract management and oversight as a warfighter task. In a March 2010 report, we noted that commanders and senior leaders often view operational contract support as a logistics problem or a contracting problem and not as a responsibility of the entire force. Most of the CORs we interviewed performed their contract duties as an additional duty to their military responsibilities. As a result, these CORs said they did not always have the time to complete their oversight responsibilities or that not enough CORs were assigned to a contract to provide sufficient oversight. In fact, some commanders and other personnel we interviewed questioned the idea that units should be responsible for contract oversight, and believed that contract oversight should be provided by other organizations. While DOD is experiencing a shortage of CORs in Afghanistan, the amount of money spent on contracts has increased as evidenced by the increase in reported DOD obligations for contracts—from $11 billion in fiscal year 2010 to $16 billion in fiscal year 2011. Additionally, the turnover rate of CORs is high due to unit rotations, frequently leaving gaps in contract coverage. Based on guidance from the Commander of the International Security Assistance Force and United States Forces-Afghanistan issued in September 2010,[46] even more personnel are needed to oversee contracts as a result of this increase.

Conclusions

DOD and the services have taken some steps, such as developing a new CORs training course with a focus on contingency operations to improve oversight of contracts in contingency operations, such as in Afghanistan; other more general efforts, such as the COR certification program for services' acquisitions, may also lead to improvement. However, in our work in Afghanistan we found that CORs are still not fully prepared to oversee the multitude of contracts for which they are assigned, potentially resulting in a significant waste of taxpayer dollars and an increased risk to the success of operations. The current mechanism for training CORs that also perform duties related to the requirements determination process and to the development of requirements documentation continues to have weaknesses because DOD has not yet developed training standards to ensure that these personnel fully understand Joint Operational Area specific issues such as the Afghan First program, the Counterinsurgency Contracting Guidance, and the details on the preparation of statements of work and documents required by the contract review boards. As noted in an Army Contracting Command publication, what contracting organizations do and how they do it cannot be foreign to the warfighter. Military personnel such as commanders, senior leaders, CORs, and other personnel expected to have a role in operational contract support are often not familiar with their contract roles and responsibilities until they reach theater because DOD has not sufficiently expanded the professional military education curriculum and provided more training on contract support with a particular emphasis on contingency operations. Further, having an insufficient number of CORs with the appropriate

---

[46] Commander, International Security Assistance Force/United States Forces - Afghanistan, *COMISAF's Counterinsurgency (COIN) Contracting Guidance* (Sept. 8, 2010).

subject area-related technical expertise or access to dedicated subject matter experts in specialty areas hinders DOD's ability to ensure that operational units obtain vital supplies and services when needed. Moreover, contract management and oversight has become more challenging due to a shortage of oversight personnel, an increase in the number of contracts, a high personnel turnover rate, training burden challenges, and an increase in the complexity of the work contracted. All of these have resulted in delays and errors in the procurement process. Further, as a result of these workload constraints, military personnel serving as CORs are limited in the number of contracts that they can reasonably manage and oversee considering the technical nature and complexity of each contract. Given DOD's heavy reliance on contractors during operations in Afghanistan and given the unpredictability of potential future contingencies, it is critical that DOD address these challenges as soon as possible to mitigate the risk to the success of operations, to obtain reasonable assurance that contractors are meeting their contract requirements and that troops are getting what they need to support contingency operations, and to help ensure that tax dollars are not being wasted.

Recommendations for Executive Action

To provide for improved oversight of operational contract support, we are recommending that DOD enhance the current strategy for providing contract management and oversight in Afghanistan and other areas of operations. Specifically, we recommend that the Secretary of Defense take the following four actions:

- Direct the CENTCOM Commander in consultation with the Secretaries of the military departments to develop standards for training to ensure that CORs are fully trained on the contract support in Afghanistan, to include information on the Afghan First program, Counterinsurgency Contracting Guidance, and details on the preparation of statements of work and documents required by the contract review boards.
- Direct the Chairman of the Joint Chiefs of Staff and the Secretaries of the military departments to fully institutionalize operational contract support in professional military education to ensure that CORs, commanders, senior leaders, and other personnel expected to perform operational contract support duties are prepared to do so by integrating and expanding the curriculum and by increasing the number of training offerings on operational contract support with a particular emphasis on contingency operations.

- Direct the Under Secretary of Defense for Acquisition, Technology, and Logistics in consultation with the appropriate CENTCOM officials to establish and maintain a sufficient number of subject matter experts in specialty areas dedicated to the CENTCOM Joint Theater Support Contracting Command to assist CORs with providing contract oversight.
- Direct the Under Secretary of Defense for Acquisition, Technology, and Logistics to develop standards regarding the number of contracts that a COR can manage and oversee based on the technical nature and complexity of the contract.

Agency Comments and Our Evaluation

We provided a draft of this report to DOD for comment. In written comments, DOD concurred with our recommendations. DOD's comments are reprinted in their entirety in appendix II. DOD also provided technical comments, which we incorporated into the report as appropriate.

DOD concurred with our recommendation that the Secretary of Defense direct the CENTCOM Commander in consultation with the Secretaries of the military departments to develop standards for training to ensure that CORs are fully trained in contract support in Afghanistan, to include information on the Afghan First program, Counterinsurgency Contracting Guidance, and details on the preparation of statements of work and documents required by the contract review boards. DOD stated that CENTCOM has identified COR training in its pre-deployment requirement for units and personnel being deployed to Afghanistan, referring to fragmentary order 09-1700, which lists theater training requirements for forces deploying to the CENTCOM area of responsibility. Although the fragmentary order identifies COR training as a training requirement for certain personnel, the wording in this order lacks the specificity to adequately prepare CORs for contract support in Afghanistan. For example, the fragmentary order does not require that CORs be trained on how to use the Afghan First Program and the Counterinsurgency Contracting Guidance and on how to prepare the statements of work and other documents required by the contract review boards. DOD further stated that CENTCOM reviewed and updated pre-deployment training requirements during a conference in early January 2012, but did not provide any specific information on what those updates entailed. DOD also stated that the COR training requirement will remain as required pre-deployment training and that an updated version of the pre-deployment requirement will be finalized and released no later than April 2012. Because DOD did not provide any specific details on what, if any, changes to training requirements will be included in its April 2012 update, we are unable evaluate the extent to which DOD's proposed actions would address our recommendations.

DOD concurred with our recommendation that the Secretary of Defense direct the Chairman of the Joint Chiefs of Staff and the Secretaries of the military departments to fully institutionalize OCS in professional military education by increasing the number of training offerings with a particular emphasis on contingency operations to ensure that CORs, commanders, senior leaders, and other personnel expected to perform OCS duties are prepared to do so. DOD stated that the Deputy Assistant Secretary of Defense for Program Support in the Office of the Under Secretary of Defense for Acquisition, Technology and Logistics and the Director of Logistics in the Joint Staff are currently engaged in a study to develop a strategy for OCS professional military education and that DOD recognizes the need for a holistic view of the entire OCS education requirement. DOD said it will assess existing professional military education to recommend OCS learning objectives for appropriate places in existing curricula. Additionally, DOD stated that the Army has recently taken major steps to improve training for commanders, senior leaders, and personnel expected to perform OCS duties. However, DOD did not describe what specific steps DOD has taken to fully institutionalize OCS in professional military education. Further, while it is commendable that DOD is developing a strategy for the OCS professional military education, DOD did not indicate when its strategy would be completed. Until DOD expands the curriculum and increases the number of training offerings on OCS, contract management and oversight in Afghanistan will continue to be hindered.

DOD concurred with our recommendation that the Secretary of Defense direct the Under Secretary of Defense for Acquisition, Technology, and Logistics in consultation with the appropriate CENTCOM officials to establish and maintain a sufficient number of subject matter experts in specialty areas dedicated to the CENTCOM Joint Theater Support Contracting Command to assist CORs with providing contract oversight. DOD stated that the Undersecretary of Defense for Acquisition, Technology, and Logistics will work through the Joint Staff to have CENTCOM identify the requirements for dedicated subject matter experts and the military departments to source these positions within budget constraints, and that the subject matter experts will be sourced through the normal requirements process. We agree that this proposed strategy has the potential to address our recommendation to establish and maintain a sufficient number of subject matter experts in specialty areas.

DOD concurred with our recommendation that the Secretary of Defense direct the Under Secretary of Defense for Acquisition, Technology, and Logistics develop standards regarding the number of contracts that a COR can manage and oversee based on the technical nature and complexity of the contract. DOD agreed that there is a limit to the number of contracts that a COR can support. Further, DOD stated that the Under Secretary of Defense for Acquisition, Technology, and Logistics will develop and publish appropriate standards based on the technical nature and complexity of the contract. We agree that these actions, if fully implemented, would address the intent of our recommendation.

We are sending copies of this report to interested congressional committees, the Secretary of Defense, the Chairman of the Joint Chief of Staff, the Under Secretary of Defense for Personnel and Readiness, the Under Secretary of Defense for Acquisition, Technology & Logistics, Secretaries of the Army, Navy and Air Force, the Commandant of the Marine Corps, and the Commander of CENTCOM. This report will be available at no charge on GAO's website, http://www.gao.gov.

If you or your staff have any questions about this report, please contact me at (404) 679-1808 or russellc@gao.gov. Contact points for our Offices of Congressional Relations and Public Affairs may be found on the last page of this letter. GAO staff who made key contributions are listed in appendix III.

Cary B. Russell,
Acting Director, Defense Capabilities and Management

List of Committees

The Honorable Carl Levin
Chairman
The Honorable John McCain
Ranking Member
Committee on Armed Services
United States Senate

The Honorable Daniel Inouye
Chairman
The Honorable Thad Cochran
Ranking Member
Subcommittee on Defense
Committee on Appropriations

United States Senate
The Honorable Howard P. McKeon
Chairman
The Honorable Adam Smith
Ranking Member
Committee on Armed Services
House of Representatives

The Honorable C.W. Bill Young
Chairman
The Honorable Norman D. Dicks
Ranking Member
Subcommittee on Defense
Committee on Appropriations
House of Representatives

Appendix I: Scope and Methodology

To determine the extent to which the required Department of Defense (DOD) training prepares contracting officer's representatives (COR) to perform their management and oversight duties in Afghanistan, we examined guidance, evaluated the content of the required training, and interviewed CORs and senior contracting personnel from over 30 defense organizations and units in Bagram, Kabul, Kandahar, and Camp Leatherneck, Afghanistan. We examined guidance such as the Joint Publication 4-10, the Defense Contingency Contracting Officer's Representative Handbook and the U.S. Central Command (CENTCOM) Joint Theater Support Contracting Command Standard Operating Procedures addressing the CORs program[1] to identify training requirements for CORs in contingency areas such as Afghanistan. To evaluate the content of the training, we attended training for CORs at Fort Carson, Colorado, and completed the Defense Acquisition University's online CORs contingency courses. We reviewed documents such as the program of instructions or course syllabus and other related training documents on the curriculum. We interviewed commanders, senior leaders, and contracting personnel from the Office of the Secretary of Defense, the Joint Staff, the combatant commands, service headquarters, the Defense Contract Management Agency, and defense universities to obtain a comprehensive understanding of what training was available for CORs in Afghanistan. To help determine what knowledge CORs needed to perform their management and oversight responsibilities, we reviewed contract-related documents such as contracts, purchase requisitions, and statements of work.

To determine the extent to which CORs have the appropriate subject area-related technical expertise to oversee contracts in Afghanistan, we reviewed the CENTCOM Joint Theater Support Contracting Command Standard Operating Procedure addressing the CORs program and the Defense Contingency Contracting Officer's Representative Handbook. We spoke with commanders, senior leaders, senior contracting personnel, and CORs in Afghanistan to understand the degree of subject area-related technical expertise possessed by CORs for contracts they were assigned to manage and the extent to which subject matter experts were available to provide technical support to CORs. We examined contract-related documents such as contracts and training transcripts to

---

[1]CENTCOM Contracting Command Standard Operating Procedure No.10-02: Contracting Officer's Representative (COR) Program (Rev. 2, June 2010).

assess the technical requirements of the contract as well as the technical background of CORs.

To determine the extent to which the number of CORs is sufficient to manage the contracts in Afghanistan, we examined the CENTCOM Joint Theater Support Contracting Command guidance and the Defense Contingency Contracting Officer's Representative Handbook to identify requirements related to the workload of CORs. We interviewed senior DOD contracting personnel and CORs to determine whether there was a sufficient number of CORs to manage the contracts in Afghanistan. In addition, we met with CORs to identify their contract workload and the nature of contracts they were assigned to manage.

We selected units to interview that would be in Afghanistan and available during the time of our visit based on input from service officials as well as status reports from the U.S. Army, the U.S. Air Force, and the U.S. Army National Guard. To facilitate our meetings with CORs and contracting personnel in Afghanistan, we developed a set of structured questions that were pre-tested and coordinated with service contracting experts to help ensure that we had solicited the appropriate responses. We selected and examined photographs of supplies and services provided to us by the DOD personnel to best illustrate the nature of the contract support issues we encountered in Afghanistan.

During our review, we visited or contacted key officials, CORs, senior contracting and other contracting personnel from DOD components and entities in the United States and in Afghanistan.

DOD Components and Entities in the United States

- Office of the Under Secretary of Defense for Personnel and Readiness, Arlington, Virginia
- Office of the Under Secretary of Defense for Acquisition, Technology, and Logistics, Defense Procurement Acquisition Policy, Arlington, Virginia
- U.S. Central Command, MacDill Air Force Base, Tampa, Florida
- U.S. Joint Forces Command, Suffolk, Virginia
- U.S. Army

  - Assistant Secretary of the Army for Acquisition, Logistics, and Technology, Arlington, Virginia
  - U.S. Army Material Command, Fort Belvoir, Virginia
  - U.S. Army Expeditionary Contracting Command, Fort Belvoir, Virginia
  - U.S. Army Forces Command, Fort McPherson, Georgia

- U.S. Army Training and Doctrine Command, Fort Monroe, Virginia
- U.S. Army Budget Office, Arlington, Virginia
- U.S. Army Acquisition, Logistics, and Technology Integration Office, Fort Lee, Virginia

- U.S. Air Force

  - U.S. Air Force, Air Force Contracting, Arlington, Virginia

- U.S. Navy

  - Navy Expeditionary Combat Command, Joint Expeditionary Base Little Creek-Fort Story, Virginia Beach, Virginia

- U.S. Marine Corps

  - U.S. Marine Corps Headquarters, Installation and Logistics Contracting Division, Arlington, Virginia
  - National Guard Bureau, Arlington, Virginia
  - Defense Contract Management Agency, Alexandria, Virginia

DOD Components and Entities in Afghanistan

Kandahar

- U.S. Forces Afghanistan, South
- Joint Sustainment Command Afghanistan
- Defense Contract Management Agency
- Logistics Civil Augmentation Program
- Regional Contracting Center
- 101th Combat Aviation Brigade
- 3rd Naval Construction Regiment
- 451st Air Expeditionary Wing
- 1st Brigade Combat Team/4th Infantry Division

Camp Leatherneck

- Defense Contract Management Agency
- Logistics Civil Augmentation Program
- Regional Support Command
- Logistics Civil Augmentation Program
- Division/Marine Headquarters Group, I Marine Expeditionary Force
- Marine Aircraft Wing Marine Logistics Group, I Marine Expeditionary Force
- Operational Contract Support team, I Marine Expeditionary Force
- C-8 Comptroller, I Marine Expeditionary Force
- Camp Leatherneck Commandant, I Marine Expeditionary Force

Kabul

- U.S. Central Contracting Command
- Defense Contract Management Agency
- Logistics Civil Augmentation Program
- Senior Contracting Officer – Afghanistan
- Task Force Spotlight
- Task Force 2010
- 717th Expeditionary Air Support Operations Squadron

Bagram

- Regional Contracting Center
- Combined Joint Task Force Four
- Defense Contract Management Agency
- Defense Contract Audit Agency
- 2nd Brigade, 34th Infantry Division
- 17th Combat Support Sustainment Brigade
- Combined Joint Task Force-101 CJ 4 & 8
- 46th Military Police

We performed our audit work from April 2010 to March 2012 in accordance with generally accepted government auditing standards. Generally accepted government auditing standards require that we plan and perform the audit to obtain sufficient, appropriate evidence to provide a reasonable basis for our findings and conclusions based on our audit objectives. We believe that the evidence obtained provides a reasonable basis for this assessment based on our audit objectives.

Appendix II: Comments from the Department of Defense

OFFICE OF THE UNDER SECRETARY OF DEFENSE
4000 DEFENSE PENTAGON
WASHINGTON, D.C. 20301-4000

MAR 12 2012

PERSONNEL AND
READINESS

Mr. Cary B. Russell
Acting Director, Capabilities and Management Team
U.S. Government Accountability Office
441 G Street, NW,
Washington, DC 20548

Dear Mr. Russell:

This is the Department of Defense response to Government Accountability Office (GAO)

Draft Report (GAO-12-290), "OPERATIONAL CONTRACT SUPPORT: Management and

Oversight Improvements Needed in Afghanistan," dated March 2012 (GAO Code 351474).

Thank you for the opportunity to comment. We concur with the GAO

recommendations. Elaboration on this position is in the enclosure appended to this letter.

Sincerely,

Laura J. Junor
Deputy Assistant Secretary of Defense
Readiness

Enclosure:
As stated

GAO Draft Report Dated March 2012
GAO-12-290 (GAO CODE 351474)

"OPERATIONAL CONTRACT SUPPORT: MANAGEMENT AND OVERSIGHT
IMPROVEMENTS NEEDED IN AFGHANISTAN"

DEPARTMENT OF DEFENSE COMMENTS
TO THE GAO RECOMMENDATIONS

RECOMMENDATION 1: The GAO recommends that the Secretary of Defense direct
the CENTCOM Commander to develop standards for training to ensure that contracting
officer's representatives (CORs) are fully trained on the contract support in Afghanistan
to include information on the Afghan First Program, Counterinsurgency Contracting
Guidance, and details on the preparation of statements of work and documents required
by the contract review boards.

DoD RESPONSE: Concur. CENTCOM has identified COR training in the Cat "C" pre-
deployment requirement for units and personnel being deployed to Afghanistan
(Reference USCENTCOM FRAGO 09-1700). Additionally, CENTCOM J7 reviewed
and updated pre-deployment training requirements during their training conference in
early January 2012. The COR requirements will remain as required pre-deployment
training for units and personnel deploying to Afghanistan. An updated version of
FRAGO 09-1700 will be finalized and released no later than April 2012.

RECOMMENDATION 2: The GAO recommends that the Secretary of Defense direct
the Chairman of the Joint Chiefs of Staff and the Secretaries of the military departments
to fully institutionalize operational contract support in professional military education to
ensure that CORs, commanders, senior leaders, and other personnel expected to perform
operational contract support duties are prepared to do so by integrating and expanding the
curriculum and by increasing the number of training offerings on operational contract
support with a particular emphasis on contingency operations.

DoD RESPONSE: Concur. The Deputy Assistant Secretary of Defense for Program
Support in the Office of the Under Secretary of Defense (Acquisition, Technology and
Logistics) and the Director of Logistics in the Joint Staff are currently engaged in a study
to develop a strategy for Operation Contract Support (OCS) professional military
education. We recognize the need for a holistic view of the entire OCS education
requirement and will assess existing professional military education to recommend OCS
learning objectives for appropriate places in existing curricula.

Additionally, the Army has recently taken some major steps to improve training for
commanders, senior leaders, and personnel expected to perform OCS duties.

RECOMMENDATION 3: The GAO recommends that the Secretary of Defense direct the Under Secretary of Defense for Acquisition, Technology, and Logistics in consultation with the appropriate CENTCOM officials to establish and maintain a sufficient number of subject matter experts in specialty areas dedicated to the CENTCOM Joint Theater Support Contracting Command to assist CORs with providing contract oversight.

DoD RESPONSE: Concur. The Undersecretary of Defense (Acquisition, Technology, and Logistics) will work through the Joint Staff to have CENTCOM identify the requirement for dedicated subject matter experts (SME) and the Military Departments to source those positions, within budget constraints. These SMEs will be sourced through the normal requirements process.

RECOMMENDATION 4: The GAO recommends that the Secretary of Defense direct the Under Secretary of Defense for Acquisition, Technology, and Logistics to develop standards regarding the number of contracts that a COR can manage and oversee based on the technical nature and complexity of the contract.

DoD RESPONSE: Concur. The Department agrees there is a limit to the number of contracts that a COR can manage and oversee. Under Secretary of Defense (Acquisition, Technology, and Logistics) will develop and publish appropriate standards based on the technical nature and complexity of the contract.

Appendix III: GAO Contact and Staff Acknowledgments

GAO Contact	Cary B. Russell, (404) 679-1808 or russellc@gao.gov.
Staff Acknowledgments	In addition to the contact named above, William Solis, Director; David Schmitt, Assistant Director; Carole Coffey, Assistant Director; Tracy Burney, Alfonso Garcia, Christopher Miller, Michael Shaughnessy and Natasha Wilder made key contributions to this report. Peter Anderson, Kenneth Cooper, Branch Delaney, Mae Jones and Amie Steele provided assistance in report preparation.

GAO's Mission	The Government Accountability Office, the audit, evaluation, and investigative arm of Congress, exists to support Congress in meeting its constitutional responsibilities and to help improve the performance and accountability of the federal government for the American people. GAO examines the use of public funds; evaluates federal programs and policies; and provides analyses, recommendations, and other assistance to help Congress make informed oversight, policy, and funding decisions. GAO's commitment to good government is reflected in its core values of accountability, integrity, and reliability.
Obtaining Copies of GAO Reports and Testimony	The fastest and easiest way to obtain copies of GAO documents at no cost is through GAO's website (www.gao.gov). Each weekday afternoon, GAO posts on its website newly released reports, testimony, and correspondence. To have GAO e-mail you a list of newly posted products, go to www.gao.gov and select "E-mail Updates."
Order by Phone	The price of each GAO publication reflects GAO's actual cost of production and distribution and depends on the number of pages in the publication and whether the publication is printed in color or black and white. Pricing and ordering information is posted on GAO's website, http://www.gao.gov/ordering.htm. Place orders by calling (202) 512-6000, toll free (866) 801-7077, or TDD (202) 512-2537. Orders may be paid for using American Express, Discover Card, MasterCard, Visa, check, or money order. Call for additional information.
Connect with GAO	Connect with GAO on Facebook, Flickr, Twitter, and YouTube. Subscribe to our RSS Feeds or E-mail Updates. Listen to our Podcasts. Visit GAO on the web at www.gao.gov.
To Report Fraud, Waste, and Abuse in Federal Programs	Contact: Website: www.gao.gov/fraudnet/fraudnet.htm E-mail: fraudnet@gao.gov Automated answering system: (800) 424-5454 or (202) 512-7470
Congressional Relations	Katherine Siggerud, Managing Director, siggerudk@gao.gov, (202) 512-4400, U.S. Government Accountability Office, 441 G Street NW, Room 7125, Washington, DC 20548
Public Affairs	Chuck Young, Managing Director, youngc1@gao.gov, (202) 512-4800 U.S. Government Accountability Office, 441 G Street NW, Room 7149 Washington, DC 20548

www.ingramcontent.com/pod-product-compliance
Lightning Source LLC
Chambersburg PA
CBHW080922290526
45795CB00007BA/2627

9 781492 297871